RHINOS

By Melissa Cole
Photographs by Tom and Pat Leeson

BLACKBIRCH®
PRESS

THOMSON
GALE

San Diego • Detroit • New York • San Francisco • Cleveland • New Haven, Conn. • Waterville, Maine • London • Munich

For more information, contact
The Gale Group, Inc.
27500 Drake Rd.
Farmington Hills, MI 48331-3535
Or you can visit our Internet site at http://www.gale.com

Photo Credits: Cover, all photos © Tom and Pat Leeson Nature Wildlife Photography; back cover © CORBIS; pages 3, 12, 19 © McDonald Wildlife Photography

LIBRARY OF CONGRESS CATALOGING-IN-PUBLICATION DATA

Cole, Melissa S.
    Rhinos / by Melissa S. Cole.
        p. cm. — (wild Africa series)
    Summary: Describes the social interactions of rhinos, their eating habits, mating, and encounters with humans.
    ISBN 1-56711-633-7 (hardback : alk. paper)
    1. Rhinoceroses—Juvenile literature. [1. Rhinoceroses. 2. Endangered species.] I. Title.
    QL737.U63 C65 2003
    599.66'8—dc21   2002003226

Printed in China
10 9 8 7 6 5 4 3 2 1

Contents

Introduction 4

The Rhino's Body. 6

Special Features 8

Social Life. 11

Feeding 15

The Mating Game 18

Raising Young. 19

Rhinos and Humans 22

Introduction

Rhinoceroses (rhinos) have lived on earth for millions of years. Fossils, or bones of more than 100 species of rhinos have been found in North America, Europe, Africa, and Asia. Only five species of rhinos exist today. Indian, Javan, and Sumatran rhinos live in Asia. White and black rhinos live in Africa.

There are only five species of rhinos left in the world.

The Rhino's Body

All 5 species of rhinos have large, barrel-shaped bodies. They have strong, stout legs. Rhinos do not have much fat on their bodies. Their bulk consists mainly of large groups of muscles attached to thick bones. Rhinos are extremely powerful animals. They are able to defend themselves against lions and knock down trees. The can even flip cars over! Rhinos look like they would be slow and clumsy—but an angry rhino can charge at speeds faster than 30 miles (48 km) per hour! Rhinos can run fast for a long distance without stopping.

Rhinos can run very fast despite their large bodies.

White rhinos are larger than black rhinos. White rhino males, or bulls, average 5 to 6 feet (1.5 –1.8 m) tall. They weigh more than 5,000 pounds (2,268 kg). Black rhino bulls are 5 feet (1.5 m) tall at the shoulder. They weigh 2,000 to 3,000 pounds (907.2–1,360.8 kg). Both rhino males are usually larger than females, called cows.

Rhinos have thick, wrinkly, grayish-colored skin. Even though rhino skin seems tough, it is sensitive. Rhinos roll in mud, dust, and sand to coat their skin. This protects it from thorns, biting insects, and sunburn. Small birds, called oxpeckers or tickbirds, often sit on rhinos' backs. These birds pick parasites off of rhinos' skin. An African rhino's skin is almost hairless. Only the tip of its tail, its eyelashes, and the rims of its ears have hair.

White rhinos (top) are larger than black rhinos (bottom).

Special Features

Rhinoceroses get their name from the Greek words *rhino* (nose) and *keras* (horn). A rhinoceros may grow one or two horns. These horns are attached to the skin of its nose, one in front of the other. The back horn is usually smaller. Unlike other animals' horns, a rhino's horns are not made of bone. Rhino horns are made of keratin. This substance is also found in hooves, fingernails, and hair.

Rhinos keep their horns sharp by rubbing them on rocks or trees. If a rhino's horn gets knocked off, it will grow back at a rate of about 2 inches (5 cm) per year. African rhinos grow the longest horns. A white rhino's front horn often grows more than 6 feet (1.8 m) tall! A black rhino's front horn grows an average of 4 feet (1.2 m) tall. Back horns usually grow between 14 and 16 inches (35.6–40.6 cm)long.

Rhinos have sharp horns.

Rhinos use their horns in many ways. They can break tree limbs to reach tender leaves to eat. During the dry season, they use their horns to dig in the ground. They search for juicy roots and underground water. An angry rhino can use its horn to stab and toss enemies, such as lions and hyenas, into the air!

Rhinos have weak eyesight. Therefore, they and cannot see faraway objects clearly. A rhino's eyes are on each side of its head, instead of facing forward. A rhino must turn its head and use one eye at a time. It is difficult for rhinos to peer over their front horns. Because their eyesight is so poor, rhinos rely on their senses of smell and hearing.

A rhino uses its horn to dig up roots.

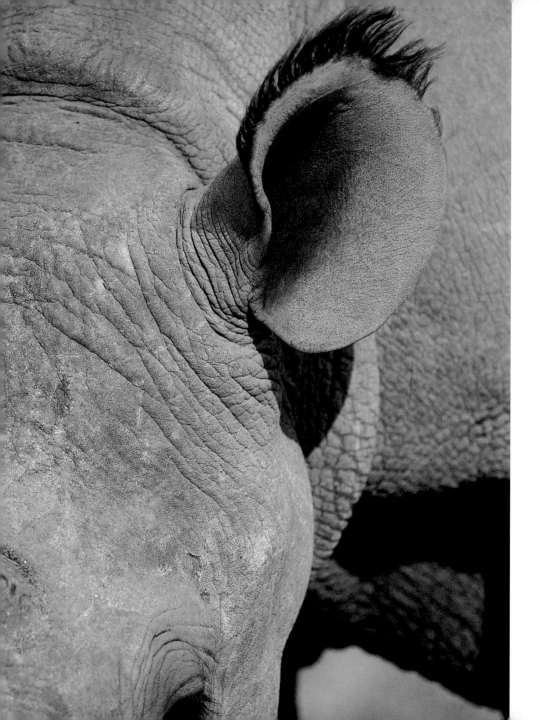

Rhinos have an excellent sense of hearing. They have small, round ears that stick up on top of their heads. Their ears can move around and pick up noises even while they are asleep.

Rhinos depend on their sharp sense of smell. They can sniff out sources of food and water, as well as other animals. If a mother rhino and her baby, or calf, are separated, they do not have to look for each other. They can put their noses to the ground and follow each other's scent until they find each other.

Rhinos have excellent hearing.

Social Life

White rhinos are more social than black rhinos. White rhinos often live in family groups. A group of rhinos is called a crash. Families can have several cows and their calves. Also included in a crash are other young rhinos. Adult males will sometimes join the group to find a mate.

Black rhinos spend most of their time alone. Mothers and calves stay together for several years. Adult rhinos briefly come together to mate, but then return to their lives on their own.

White rhinos form family groups.

Scientists who study rhinos have found that each rhino has its own separate area, or home range. This is where it feeds, drinks, and sleeps. The size of a home range depends on the food and water supply. When there is enough to eat and plenty of water, a home range may only be one mile (1.6 km) square. During the dry season, when there is less food and water, a territory may be as large as 50 square miles (80.5 km).

Rhinos greet each other by touching with their noses.

White rhino territories often overlap. When females meet, they greet each other with a friendly nose nuzzle. When two males come together, they may snort, paw the ground, and push each other nose to nose. They do this until one rhino backs off. Black rhinos have larger home ranges than white rhinos do, so they rarely have these run-ins.

Rhinos communicate using sounds and gestures. Angry rhinos curl their tails up and growl or snort. If they are ready to attack, they paw the ground, lower their heads, and flatten their ears. Calves and mothers call to each other with high pitched sounds.

Scientists also have found that rhinos can call each other with special infrasonic sounds. These noises are too low for humans to hear. And they can travel long distances.

Scent is very important to rhino communication. Bulls mark territory by spreading their scent around its edges. They walk around the edges of their territory each day and spray urine on trees, rocks, and bushes. This lets other rhinos know that the territory is occupied.

Rhinos also communicate using dung, or droppings. When a rhino comes upon the dung of another rhino, it leaves its own droppings on the dung heap. Each rhino that passes by adds to the pile. Eventually, there is a huge heap of dung—3 feet (.9 m) high and over 16 feet (4.9 m) wide! Rhinos sniff the dung, walk through it, kick it, and scatter it about. Since each animal has its own scent, rhinos can tell how many other rhinos are in the area. They know what their sex is, and if a female is ready to mate, just by checking out the local dung heap!

A male rhino will mark territory with its scent.

Feeding

Rhinos travel from feeding areas to water holes along well-worn paths. Most rhinos feed early in the morning. They nap during the hottest part of the day. They sleep under shady trees if they can find them. Rhinos usually rest standing up. But they will lie on their stomachs to sleep for longer periods of time. In the late afternoons, rhinos roll in mud near water holes. They feed again during the evenings when it is cooler.

Rhinos are herbivores, or plant eaters. They eat about 50 pounds (22.8 kg) of vegetation per day. They chew their food with large, ridged teeth called molars. All rhinos have 12 to 14 pairs of these teeth.

Rhinos like to eat early in the morning.

Black and white rhinos eat different types of plants. White rhinos are grazers. They eat mainly short grasses and herbs. They spend most of their time on flat, grassy plains called savannas. Black rhinos are browsers. They nibble on tree bark, leaves, fruit, and shrubs. They usually live in wooded areas. Here, they can find low shrubs and trees.

One way to tell white and black rhinos apart is by their lips.

Black rhinos have pointy upper lips that they use to pull up plants to eat.

White rhinos have wide, square lips. They use their upper lips to rip up large mouthfuls of grass. Black rhinos have a pointy upper lip that acts like a small finger. Black rhinos can use their flexible upper lips to grasp leaves and twigs. And then they can stuff food into their mouths.

Rhinos must drink plenty of water to survive. They drink between 15 to 25 gallons (56.8–94.6 L) of water per day. In times of drought, when there is no water, rhinos can go 5 days without drinking. Sometimes rhinos feed on water bearing plants to get enough water. They also dig holes in the ground with their front feet and horns to reach underground water.

A rhino must drink a lot of water to survive.

The Mating Game

Rhinos can mate any time of the year. Females who are ready to mate spray urine wherever they go to signal males in the area. They also make whistling sounds to attract males. Female rhinos are usually ready to mate when they are 3 years old. But they may not have their first baby until they are 5 or 6 years old. Bulls are able to reproduce when they are between 7 and 9 years old.

Black rhinos rarely fight to get a cow's attention. White rhinos, however, fight fiercely over females. They snort and scream, crash into each other, and lock horns. Usually the stronger bull wins. The other bull will leave in defeat. The winner then gets a chance to mate with a willing female.

Courting rhinos sometimes nuzzle each other gently. But they are often noisy and violent. Cows have been known to attack bulls and jab them with their horns. Mating rhinos only stay together for a few days. The bull does not help the cow raise the calf.

Bulls and cows only stay together for a few days to mate.

Raising Young

Females have gestation period, or pregnancy, that lasts about 15 months for black rhinos and 16 months for white rhinos. A cow often finds a quiet, hidden place to have her calf. She gives birth standing up. After it is born, the cow licks a calf to clean it.

Rhino calves are able to walk shortly after being born.

Baby rhinos are about 2 feet (.6 m) tall when they are born. White rhino calves weigh between 100 to 150 pounds (45–68 kg) and black rhino babies weigh between 60 and 90 pounds (27–40 kg). Calves can stand up within an hour of being born. They are also able to walk within 2 hours.

Calves begin to nurse within their first hours of life. During their first 4 months, calves gain about 2 1/2 pounds (1.1 kg) each day. When calves are 2 weeks old, they begin to nibble on plants and grasses. Calves continue to nurse for one to two years.

Calves are born with thick skin on the ends of their noses. This is where the horn, or horns, will grow. At 8 months old, the front horn is about 3 inches (7.6 cm) long and the second horn is about one inch (2.5 cm) high.

Rhinos mothers will do everything possible to protect their calves. Black rhino calves generally walk behind their mothers. White rhinos place their babies a few steps in front of them. This difference in behavior is probably due to their habitat. Black rhino mothers clear a path through the low shrubs and bushes. This makes it easier for their calves to walk. These mothers also lead the way in case a predator is hiding behind the bushes. White rhinos live in open grasslands, so clearing a path for their young is not necessary. It also is easier for a white rhino to watch for danger with her calf in front of her.

Hyenas, leopards, crocodiles, and sometimes lions attack baby rhinos. When threatened, a mother rhino turns her body sideways. This blocks the predator's path to the calf. Mother rhinos are fierce. They will even charge an adult lion to defend their babies. If a group of white rhinos is together when a predator appears, cows stand in a circle around the calves with their horns facing outwards.

Rhino cows teach their young how to defend themselves. They also show their calves which plants to eat, how to wallow in mud, and where to find water. When a calf is 2 to 5 years old, it often is forced to leave when its mother mates, or when a new calf is born. A calf may join other older calves or childless females until it is grown. When a calf is 3 years old, it is almost as big as its mother. Though, it is not fully grown until it is about 7 years old. Rhinos can live about 35 years in the wild.

White rhinos live in open grasslands.

Rhinos and Humans

An international law bans the trade of rhino horns. Still, humans hunt rhinos. Their horns are ground up and used in traditional medicines in China and Korea. Rhino horns also are in great demand in northern Yemen. Here, they are carved into handles for special knives. Buyers are willing to pay more than $30,000 per pound (.5 kg) for rhino horns—that is more than the price of gold! This demand makes it difficult to stop the illegal poaching, or hunting, of rhinos.

Some African countries have tried to stop poachers by capturing rhinos and sawing off their horns. This solution has not worked well. Their horns repeatedly grow back. And poachers kill de-horned rhinos anyway, because the stump itself is valuable.

In some areas, poaching is so difficult to control that armed guards are on a 24-hour watch. Electric fences aimed at keeping poachers out surround some sanctuaries. Here, rhinos can live and breed in safety.

In 1970, about 65,000 black rhinos lived throughout Africa. Today, there are between 2,500 and 2,700 black rhinos left there. There are approximately 7,000 white rhinos still living in Africa. Zoos are actively trying to breed rhinos to save them from disappearing. People must protect rhinos from poachers. They also must set aside safe habitats where rhinos can live natural lives.

There are only about 7,000 white rhinos living in Africa today.

Rhino Facts

Scientific Name: White rhinos: ceratotherium simium; Black rhinos: diceros bicornis

Shoulder Height: White rhinos: 5–6 feet (1.5–1.8 m); Black rhinos: 4–5.5 feet (1.4–1.7 m)

Weight: White rhinos: 4,000–6,000 pounds (1,800–2,100 kg); Black rhinos: 1,750–3,000 pounds (800–1,350 kg)

Color: Gray

Reaches sexual maturity at: females at 3 years old; males at 7–9 years old

Gestation (pregnancy period): 15-16 months

Litter Size: one calf

Favorite Food: grass, leaves, fruit

Range: White and black rhinos live in the bushes and savannas of Africa.

Glossary

Crash A group of rhinos

Gestation period The length of time during which a female is pregnant

Infrasonic sounds Noises that are too low for humans to hear

Keratin The substance that forms horns, hair, hooves, and fingernails

Migrate To move from one area to another

Poach To illegally hunt an animal

Territory An area, or home range, where an animal spends most of its time

Further Reading

Books

Lavine, Sigmund A. *Wonders of Rhino.* New York: Dodd, Mead and Co., 1982.

Schlaepfer, Gloria G. and Samuelson, Marylou. *The African Rhinos.* New York: Dillon Press, 1992.

Walker, Sally M. *Rhinos.* Minneapolis: CarolRhoda Publishing, 1996.

Watt, Melanie E. *Black Rhinos.* Austin: Raintree Steck-Vaughn, 1998.

Web sites

Rhino Facts

http://www.midsouth.rr.com/zoo/zooipix/rhinofacts.html

WWF International Rhino Page

http://www.panda.org/resources/publications/species/african_rhino/index.html

Index

Crash, 11

Drinking, 17

Feeding, 15

Home range, 12
Hunting, 22

Keratin, 8

Mating, 11, 14, 18

Nursing, 19

Oxpeckers, 7

Poaching, 22-23

Predators, 20

Rhinos,
Body, 6
Communication, 12-13, 18
Droppings, 13-14
Ears, 10, 13
Eyesight, 9

Gestation period, 19
Hearing, 10
Horns, 8-9, 19, 22
Lips, 16
Scent, 10, 13
Skin, 7, 19

Savannas, 16